I0448153

July 2013

OVERSTAY ENFORCEMENT

Additional Actions Needed to Assess DHS's Data and Improve Planning for a Biometric Air Exit Program

OVERSTAY ENFORCEMENT

Additional Actions Needed to Assess DHS's Data and Improve Planning for a Biometric Air Exit Program

GAO Highlights

Highlights of GAO-13-683, a report to congressional requesters

Why GAO Did This Study

Each year, millions of visitors come to the United States legally on a temporary basis either with or without a visa. Overstays are individuals who were admitted legally on a temporary basis but then overstayed their authorized periods of admission. DHS has primary responsibility for identifying and taking enforcement action to address overstays. In April 2011, GAO reported on DHS's actions to identify and address overstays and made recommendations to strengthen these processes. DHS concurred and has taken or is taking steps to address them. DHS has also reported taking further actions to address overstays.

GAO was asked to review DHS's progress since April 2011. This report addresses (1) DHS's efforts to review its records to identify potential overstays, (2) the extent to which DHS's changes in its systems or processes have improved data on potential overstays and DHS's ability to report overstay rates, and (3) the extent to which DHS has made progress toward establishing a biometric exit system. GAO analyzed DHS overstay data and documents—such as those related to the overstay identification processes and biometric exit plans—and interviewed relevant DHS officials.

What GAO Recommends

GAO recommends that DHS assess and document the reliability of its data, and establish time frames and milestones for a biometric air exit evaluation framework. DHS concurred with the recommendations.

View GAO-13-683. For more information, contact Rebecca Gambler at (202) 512-8777 or gamblerr@gao.gov.

What GAO Found

Since April 2011, the Department of Homeland Security (DHS) has taken action to address a backlog of potential overstay records that GAO previously identified. Specifically, DHS reviewed such records to identify national security and public safety threats, but unmatched arrival records—those without corresponding departure records—remain in DHS's system. GAO had previously reported that, as of January 2011, DHS had a backlog of 1.6 million unmatched arrival records that had not been reviewed through automated or manual processes. DHS tracks arrivals and departures and closes records for individuals with matching arrival and departure records. Unmatched arrival records indicate that the individual is a potential overstay. In 2011, DHS reviewed this backlog of 1.6 million records, closed about 863,000 records, and removed them from the backlog. As new unmatched arrival records have accrued, DHS has continued to review all of these new records for national security and public safety concerns. As of June 2013, DHS's unmatched arrival records totaled more than 1 million.

DHS has actions completed and under way to improve data on potential overstays and report overstay rates, but the effect of these improvements is not yet known. Further, DHS continues to face challenges in reporting reliable overstay rates. DHS has streamlined connections among databases used to identify potential overstays. However, these improvements do not address some underlying data quality issues, such as missing land departure data. Federal law requires DHS to report overstay estimates, but DHS or its predecessor has not regularly done so since 1994. In April 2011, GAO reported that DHS officials said that they have not reported overstay rates because DHS has not had sufficient confidence in the quality of its overstay data. In February 2013, the Secretary of Homeland Security testified that DHS plans to report overstay rates by December 2013. However, DHS has not assessed or documented improvements in the reliability of data used to develop overstay estimates, in accordance with federal internal control standards. Without such a documented assessment to ensure the reliability of these data, decision makers would not have the information needed to use these data for policy-making purposes.

Developing and implementing a biometric exit capability to collect biometric data, such as fingerprints, which is required by federal law, has been a long-standing challenge for DHS. In May 2012, DHS internally reported recommendations to support the planning for a biometric exit capability at airports—DHS's priority for biometric exit capabilities—that could also be implemented at seaports in the future; however, as of June 2013, DHS's planning did not address a biometric exit capability at land ports of entry. DHS officials stated that the department's goal is to develop information and report to Congress about the benefits and costs of biometric air exit options before the fiscal year 2016 budget cycle. Standard practices for project management state that time frames should be documented as part of the planning process; however, DHS has a high-level plan for a biometric air exit capability, and it does not clearly define the steps, time frames, and milestones needed to develop and implement an evaluation framework, as recommended in DHS's May 2012 report. Without robust planning that includes time frames and milestones, DHS does not have reasonable assurance that it will meet its time frame for developing and implementing an evaluation framework.

_____ **United States Government Accountability Office**

Contents

Figures

Abbreviations

ADIS	Arrival and Departure Information System
ATS	Automated Targeting System
CBP	U.S. Customs and Border Protection
CLAIMS	Computer-Linked Application Information Management System 3
CTCEU	Counterterrorism and Criminal Exploitation Unit
DHS	Department of Homeland Security
ERO	Enforcement and Removal Operations
HSI	Homeland Security Investigations
ICE	U.S. Immigration and Customs Enforcement
IDENT	Automated Biometric Identification System
OAU	Overstay Analysis Unit
OBIM	Office of Biometric Identity Management
S&T	Science and Technology Directorate
SEVIS	Student and Exchange Visitor Information System
US-VISIT	U.S. Visitor and Immigrant Status Indicator Technology Program

GAO U.S. GOVERNMENT ACCOUNTABILITY OFFICE

441 G St. N.W.
Washington, DC 20548

July 30, 2013

The Honorable Tom Coburn, M.D.
Ranking Member
Committee on Homeland Security and Governmental Affairs
United States Senate

The Honorable Candice S. Miller
Chairman
The Honorable Sheila Jackson Lee
Ranking Member
Subcommittee on Border and Maritime Security
Committee on Homeland Security
House of Representatives

The Honorable Susan Collins
United States Senate

The Honorable Henry Cuellar
House of Representatives

Each year, millions of visitors come to the United States legally on a temporary basis either with a visa or, in some cases, as visitors who were allowed to enter without a visa.[1] Overstays are individuals who were admitted into the country legally on a temporary basis but then overstayed their authorized periods of admission.[2] We have previously reported that most overstays are likely motivated by economic opportunities to stay in the United States beyond their authorized periods

---

[1]Visitors who are allowed to seek admission without a visa include citizens of Canada and the British Overseas Territory of Bermuda (and certain residents of other adjacent islands, such as the Bahamas) under certain circumstances, as well as Visa Waiver Program participants. This program allows nationals from certain countries to apply for admission to the United States as temporary visitors for business or pleasure without first obtaining a visa from a U.S. consulate abroad. Currently, there are 37 participants in the program.

[2]In this report, we include out-of-status students—student visa holders who fail to meet certain requirements, such as enrolling in a qualified education program—in our definition of overstays. In general, foreign students remain in status and therefore eligible to stay in the United States under their student visas as long as they are enrolled in and attending a qualified education program or engaging in authorized practical training following completion of studies.

of admission.[3] However, overstays could pose homeland security concerns—for example, 5 of the 19 September 11, 2001, hijackers were overstays.

The Department of Homeland Security (DHS) has primary responsibility for identifying and taking enforcement action to address overstays. Within DHS, U.S. Customs and Border Protection (CBP) is tasked with, among other duties, inspecting all people applying for entry to the United States to determine their admissibility to the country and screening Visa Waiver Program applicants to determine their eligibility to travel to the United States under the program. U.S. Immigration and Customs Enforcement (ICE) is the lead agency for enforcing immigration law in the interior of the United States and is primarily responsible for overstay enforcement. Within ICE's Homeland Security Investigations (HSI) directorate, the Overstay Analysis Unit is responsible for reviewing records of potential overstays and providing the results of these reviews to ICE's Counterterrorism and Criminal Exploitation Unit (CTCEU), which is responsible for initiating overstay investigations. Since 2004, DHS has collected biometric data, such as fingerprints, from travelers as part of an effort to comply with legislative requirements to track nonimmigrants' entry into and exit from the United States.[4] To do so, the Office of Biometric Identity Management (OBIM), within DHS's National Protection and Programs Directorate, manages the Arrival and Departure Information System (ADIS), which tracks and matches arrival and departure records for the purpose of identifying potential overstays, and the Automated Biometric Identification System (IDENT), which maintains biometric information that DHS collects from nonimmigrants upon their entry into the United States.[5]

---

[3]GAO, *Visa Waiver Program: Limitations with Department of Homeland Security's Plan to Verify Departure of Foreign Nationals*, GAO-08-458T (Washington, D.C.: Feb. 28, 2008).

[4]See 8 U.S.C. §§ 1365a, 1365b.

[5]IDENT also contains fingerprints collected by the Department of State to establish and verify the identities of visa applicants. Both the Overstay Analysis Unit and OBIM were formerly part of the U.S. Visitor and Immigrant Status Indicator Technology Program (US-VISIT) within DHS's National Protection and Programs Directorate. DHS initiated US-VISIT in 2003 to develop a comprehensive entry and exit system to collect biometric data from aliens traveling through U.S. ports of entry. Pursuant to the fiscal year 2013 DHS appropriations act and its accompanying explanatory statement, DHS realigned US-VISIT's overstay analysis function into ICE and created OBIM effective March 27, 2013.

In April 2011, we reported on DHS's actions to identify and take actions to address overstays and made recommendations to the department to strengthen those efforts.[6] DHS concurred with our recommendations and has taken or is taking steps to address them, as discussed later in this report. In addition, we have issued a number of reports since 2004 on DHS's collection of biometric data from nonimmigrants upon their entry into the United States, as well as the department's efforts to collect biometric data to track their exit from the country. Relying on some of this work conducted from 2007 through 2010, we made recommendations to DHS to improve planning for and implementation of a biometric exit system.[7] DHS generally concurred with our recommendations in these reports and has taken action to address a number of them, as also discussed later in this report. In addition to taking actions in response to the recommendations we have made, since April 2011, DHS has reported taking other actions to strengthen its processes for identifying and taking enforcement action against overstays, such as enhancing its use of biographic data to identify overstays and developing plans to capture biometric data as part of departure records to comply with federal law.[8]

You asked us to review actions taken by DHS to identify and address potential overstays since our April 2011 report. This report addresses (1) DHS's efforts to review records that are maintained in its databases to identify potential overstays, (2) the extent to which DHS's changes in its systems or processes have improved data on potential overstays and DHS's ability to report overstay rates, and (3) the extent to which DHS has made progress in developing and implementing a biometric exit system.

To address the first objective, we analyzed documentation on DHS's processes to review records of potential overstays and improve overstay identification, such as ICE's standard operating procedures for reviewing

---

[6]GAO, *Overstay Enforcement: Additional Mechanisms for Collecting, Assessing, and Sharing Data Could Strengthen DHS's Efforts but Would Have Costs*, GAO-11-411 (Washington, D.C.: Apr. 15, 2011).

[7]GAO, *Homeland Security: US-VISIT Pilot Evaluations Offer Limited Understanding of Air Exit Options*, GAO-10-860 (Washington, D.C.: Aug. 10, 2010), and *Homeland Security: U.S. Visitor and Immigrant Status Program's Long-standing Lack of Strategic Direction and Management Controls Needs to Be Addressed*, GAO-07-1065 (Washington, D.C.: Aug. 31, 2007).

[8]8 U.S.C. § 1365b(d).

records of potential overstays. Specifically, we analyzed the results of DHS's 2011 review of a backlog of records of potential overstays that we identified and reported on in April 2011. We also analyzed the 1.2 million records from ADIS, as of November 2012, that represent data on individuals for whom ADIS has a record of arrival but for whom DHS has no record of departure (unmatched arrival records) at that time.[9] This was the most recent date for which DHS had compiled these records at the time we began our review. To analyze the reliability of these data on the prior backlog, as well as DHS's unmatched arrival records as of November 2012, we reviewed documentation regarding the databases used to collect these data and interviewed DHS officials familiar with the data. We determined that the data were sufficiently reliable for our purposes.

To address the second objective, we analyzed documentation on changes to DHS component agency systems, such as ADIS, to enhance the use of biographic information to identify overstays, and we interviewed DHS officials to discuss the expected results of these changes. We also analyzed agreements between the United States and Canada to exchange entry and exit data as part of the Beyond the Border initiative, through which entry into one country is treated as exit from the other, and interviewed DHS and Canada Border Services Agency officials responsible for overseeing the initiative. We also collected all available data on the results of the Beyond the Border pilot phase, which occurred from September 30, 2012, through January 15, 2013. To analyze the reliability of these data, we reviewed documentation related to the exchange of these data and interviewed OBIM, CBP, and DHS Office of Policy officials familiar with the data. We determined that the data were sufficiently reliable for our purposes. We also conducted interviews with ICE and DHS Office of Policy officials regarding the department's plans to calculate and report overstay rates using the data available in its component agency systems and evaluated those plans based on statutory requirements and standards for internal control.[10] We also

---

[9]Through ADIS, DHS has identified these records as potential overstays, but as of November 2012, DHS had not conducted manual searches through DHS and other databases to determine whether there might be evidence of departure or change of status in other databases. DHS's processes for reviewing records of potential overstays are discussed in more detail later in this report and in GAO-11-411.

[10]GAO, *Standards for Internal Control in the Federal Government*, GAO/AIMD-00-21.3.1 (Washington, D.C.: November 1999).

evaluated those plans against guidance for designing evaluations and assessing the reliability of computer-processed data.[11]

To address the third objective, we reviewed statutory requirements for a biometric exit system and analyzed DHS documents, including a May 2012 report on the status of efforts to implement biometric exit capabilities at airports that was based on analysis that DHS's Science and Technology Directorate (S&T) conducted. We compared the status of DHS's efforts against statutory requirements and standard practices for project management.[12] We also interviewed DHS Office of Policy and S&T officials regarding DHS's plans for addressing recommendations in the department's May 2012 report and other ongoing efforts to develop a biometric exit system.

We conducted this performance audit from November 2012 to July 2013 in accordance with generally accepted government auditing standards. Those standards require that we plan and perform the audit to obtain sufficient, appropriate evidence to provide a reasonable basis for our findings and conclusions based on our audit objectives. We believe that the evidence obtained provides a reasonable basis for our findings and conclusions based on our audit objectives.

Background

Process for Gaining Admission to the United States

Each year, millions of visitors come to the United States legally on a temporary basis.[13] Generally, nonimmigrants wishing to visit the United States gain permission to apply for admission to the country through one of two ways. First, those eligible for the Visa Waiver Program apply online to establish eligibility to travel under the program prior to departing for the

---

[11]GAO, *Designing Evaluations: 2012 Revision,* GAO-12-208G (Washington, D.C.: January 2012), and *Assessing the Reliability of Computer Processed Data,* GAO-09-680G (Washington, D.C.: July 2009).

[12]Project Management Institute, *A Guide to the Project Management Body of Knowledge (PMBOK® Guide), Fifth Edition,* (Newton Square, PA: 2013).

[13]Temporary visitors to the United States generally are referred to as nonimmigrants. For a listing and descriptions of nonimmigrant categories, see 8 U.S.C. § 1101(a)(15); see also 8 C.F.R. § 214.1(a)(1)-(2).

United States.[14] Second, those not eligible for the Visa Waiver Program and not otherwise exempt from the visa requirement must obtain a visa from a U.S. consular office overseas.[15] Upon arriving at a port of entry, nonimmigrants must undergo inspection by CBP officers, who determine whether or not they may be admitted into the United States. If CBP determines a nonimmigrant is admissible, he or she is granted an authorized period of admission. This period may be for a specific length of time, which CBP designates by assigning a specific "admit until" date, or for as long as the nonimmigrant maintains a particular status. For example, in general, foreign students are eligible to remain in the United States for "duration of status," meaning as long as they are enrolled in and attending a qualified education program or engaging in authorized practical training following completion of studies.

An overstay is a nonimmigrant who is legally admitted to the United States for an authorized period but remains in the country illegally after that period expired without obtaining an extension of stay or a change of status or meeting other specific conditions, such as claiming asylum.[16] This includes a nonimmigrant admitted for duration of status who fails to maintain that status, such as a student who is no longer pursuing a full course of study at an approved educational institution or engaging in authorized practical training following completion of studies. In-country overstays refer to nonimmigrants who have exceeded their authorized periods of admission and remain in the United States without lawful status, while out-of-country overstays refer to individuals who have departed the United States but who, on the basis of arrival and departure information, stayed beyond their authorized periods of admission. Federal

---

[14]Nonimmigrants eligible for the Visa Waiver Program who seek admission to the United States at a land port of entry do not apply online to establish eligibility.

[15]In certain circumstances, citizens of Canada and the British Overseas Territory of Bermuda (and certain residents of other adjacent islands, such as the Bahamas) traveling to the United States as nonimmigrants do not require a visa. See 22 C.F.R. § 41.2(a)-(f).

[16]Although overstays are sometimes referred to as visa overstays, we do not use that term in this report for two reasons. First, many nonimmigrants, such as those who enter using the Visa Waiver Program, are allowed admission into the United States for a specific period of time without visas and may overstay their authorized period of admission. Second, nonimmigrants can overstay an authorized period of admission set by a CBP officer at the border without necessarily overstaying the period of their visas because their authorized period of admission may be shorter than the period of their visas.

law establishes consequences for foreign nationals who overstay their authorized periods of admission.[17]

Federal Agencies' Roles and Responsibilities Related to Overstay Identification and Enforcement

Three DHS components and offices—CBP, ICE, and OBIM—are primarily responsible for taking action to identify and address overstays, as shown in table 1. In addition, the Department of State is responsible for ensuring that individuals who have previously overstayed and are ineligible for a visa do not receive one when applying for a visa to the United States at consular offices overseas.

Table 1: Roles and Responsibilities for Addressing Overstays

Federal agency	Overall role	Overstay responsibilities
U.S. Customs and Border Protection (CBP)	Executes policies and procedures at ports of entry for the screening of travelers and merchandise entering the United States.	Determines nonimmigrant admissibility based in part on previous overstay violations and provides an admit until date, by which time the individual must leave the country to avoid overstaying, or admits an individual for duration of status.
		Collects biographic and biometric information to document nonimmigrant entry into the country and biographic information to document nonimmigrant exit from the country.
		Responsible for implementing a biometric exit program.

[17]Nonimmigrants who overstay their authorized periods of admission are subject to removal from the United States under 8 U.S.C. § 1227(a)(1)(B)-(C). Federal law provides additional sanctions against those who overstay their lawful period of admission, including a temporary or permanent bar on readmission to the country, depending on the length of overstay, and ineligibility for future admission under the Visa Waiver Program. See 8 U.S.C. §§ 1182(a)(9)(B)-(C), 1187(a)(7). The visas of nonimmigrants who overstay become void after the conclusion of their authorized period of stay, and the State Department will not issue them a new visa if they are subject to a statutory bar on readmission, unless DHS grants a waiver; if the length of overstay is not sufficient to trigger one of the bars on readmission and they are not otherwise ineligible for a visa, they may be able to obtain a new visa and CBP may readmit them to the country, if they are not otherwise inadmissble at the time they apply for readmission at a port of entry. See 8 U.S.C. §§ 1202(g), 1201, 1182(a), 1225(b); 6 U.S.C. § 236(b)-(c).

GAO-13-683 Overstay Enforcement

Federal agency	Overall role	Overstay responsibilities
U.S. Immigration and Customs Enforcement (ICE) Homeland Security Investigations (HSI) Overstay Analysis Unit (OAU) Counterterrorism and Criminal Exploitation Unit (CTCEU) HSI field offices	HSI: Investigate a range of domestic and international activities arising from the illegal movement of people and goods into, within, and out of the United States.	OAU: Identifies overstays by matching arrival and departure data and performing overstay analysis previously performed by the United States Visitor and Immigrant Status Indicator Technology (US-VISIT) program.[a] CTCEU: Identifies overstays, including potential national security risks and out of status students, and then assigns leads for further investigation by field offices. HSI field offices: Investigate overstay cases and determine appropriate action to be taken, including initiating administrative procedures to remove an individual from the country, if appropriate.
ICE Enforcement and Removal Operations (ERO)	ERO: Identifies and apprehends aliens who are subject to removal from the country, detains these individuals when necessary, and removes them from the United States.	ERO: Contributes indirectly to overstay efforts through various programs, such as the Criminal Alien Program and the Fugitive Operations Support Center.[b] Responsible for the removal of deportable aliens from the United States.
National Protection and Programs Directorate-Office of Biometric Identity Management	Stores biometric identities and matches them against derogatory information.	Manages the Automated Biometric Identification System and the Arrival and Departure Information System as previously performed by US-VISIT. Conducts recurrent matching against derogatory information and provides other biometric expertise and services.

Source: GAO analysis of DHS information.

[a]DHS initiated US-VISIT in 2003 to develop a comprehensive entry and exit system to collect biometric data from aliens traveling through U.S. ports of entry. In March 2013, DHS realigned US-VISIT's overstay analysis function into ICE.

[b]The Criminal Alien Program identifies, processes, and removes criminal aliens incarcerated throughout the United States, focusing on those that pose a risk to public safety. The Fugitive Operations Support Center operates under the National Fugitive Operations Program and reviews certain records of potential overstays generated by CTCEU to determine if any pertain to individuals that meet ERO's enforcement priorities.

Federal agencies use various databases to determine whether nonimmigrants have potentially overstayed their authorized periods of admission to the United States. As shown in table 2, several databases, in particular, provide key information on foreign nationals' arrival in and departure from the United States, foreign nationals' applications to change status once in the United States, and the status of foreign students.

Table 2: Key Federal Databases Used for Identifying Overstays

Database	Agency responsible for managing the database	Information maintained in the database related to overstays
Arrival and Departure Information System	Office of Biometric Identity Management	Nonimmigrant arrival and departure information, the date until which an individual may remain in the United States, and various other information (e.g., the address where the individual will reside in the United States)
Automated Biometric Identification System	Office of Biometric Identity Management	Biometric information collected from nonimmigrants upon their entry into the United States (i.e., fingerprints and photographs)
Student and Exchange Visitor Information System	U.S. Immigration and Customs Enforcement	Information about nonimmigrant foreign students and their programs of study and exchange visitors in the United States
Computer-Linked Application Information Management System 3 (CLAIMS) Electronic Immigration System (ELIS)	U.S. Citizenship and Immigration Services	Status of foreign nationals' petitions for extensions of stay or changes of immigration status (e.g., to convert from a tourist to a student). CLAIMS and ELIS both maintain data on applications to extend or change nonimmigrant status, and CLAIMS also maintains data on applications for work authorization or for lawful permanent resident status.

Source: GAO analysis of DHS information.

Note: In addition to the systems mentioned in this table, which we discuss later in this report, CBP's TECS system is used at ports of entry to verify traveler information and contains lookouts—electronic alerts—for certain individuals (e.g., overstays). TECS also interfaces with other agencies' databases to share this information.

Process for Identifying Overstays

ICE primarily analyzes biographic entry and exit data collected at land, air, and sea ports of entry to identify potential overstays. ICE identifies both in-country and out-of-country overstays by analyzing and comparing biographic data maintained in ADIS against information in other databases to find matches that demonstrate that a nonimmigrant may have, for instance, departed the country or filed an application to change status and thus is not an overstay. In particular, ICE analysts use ADIS to identify arrival records for which the subject's admit until date has passed and for whom DHS does not have a corresponding departure record (unmatched arrival records), which may indicate that the subject of the record is an in-country overstay.[18] For these records of potential

---

[18]ADIS may not record arrivals for travelers from Canada or Mexico who present certain documents upon arrival—for example, travelers with a Canadian legal permanent resident card—and therefore, these individuals may not be identified through the process described here for identifying potential overstays.

overstays, ICE analysts conduct automated searches, such as searching for immigration benefit application information through U.S. Citizenship and Immigration Services. ICE analysts also determine whether the subject of the record meets ICE's overstay enforcement priorities based on national security and public safety criteria. ICE prioritizes investigation of overstay leads based on the perceived risk each lead is likely to pose to national security and public safety as determined by threat analysis. In order to prioritize investigation of overstay leads, ICE uses an automated system to assign each overstay lead a priority ranking based on threat intelligence information. For the records that meet ICE's overstay enforcement priorities, ICE analysts then conduct manual searches of other databases to determine, for example, if the individual applied for refugee or asylum status. For these priority records, if ICE analysts are unable to identify evidence of a departure or a change in status, they search for the nonimmigrant's current U.S. address, and if they are able to identify an address, they send the lead to the relevant ICE HSI field office for investigation.

For cases in which ICE's analysis shows that a nonimmigrant visa holder departed the United States after the admit until date—an out-of-country overstay—and the departure was more than 90 days after the nonimmigrant's authorized period of admission expired, ICE creates a lookout that CBP officers at ports of entry and State Department officials at overseas consulates can access to determine whether that nonimmigrant is eligible for readmission at ports of entry or can receive a new visa upon application at a U.S. consulate.

Comprehensive Biometric Entry and Exit System

Beginning in 1996, federal law has required the implementation of an integrated entry and exit data system for foreign nationals.[19] Additionally, the Immigration and Naturalization Service Data Management Improvement Act of 2000 required implementation of an integrated entry and exit data system for foreign nationals that would provide access to and integrate foreign national arrival and departure data that are authorized or required to be created or collected under law and are in an electronic format in certain databases, such as those used at ports of entry and consular offices.[20] In 2003, DHS initiated the US-VISIT program

---

[19]Pub. L. No. 104-208, div. C, § 110, 110 Stat. 3009-546, 3009-558 to 59.

[20]8 U.S.C. § 1365a(b)(1).

to develop a comprehensive entry and exit system to collect biometric data from aliens traveling through United States ports of entry. In 2004, US-VISIT initiated the first step of this program by collecting biometric data on aliens entering the United States at 115 airports and 14 sea ports. The Intelligence Reform and Terrorism Prevention Act of 2004 required the Secretary of Homeland Security to develop a plan to accelerate full implementation of an automated biometric entry and exit data system that matches available information provided by foreign nationals upon their arrival in and departure from the United States.[21]

Since 2004, we have issued a number of reports on DHS's efforts to implement a biometric entry and exit system. For example, in February and August 2007, we found that DHS had not adequately defined and justified its proposed expenditures for exit pilots and demonstration projects and that it had not developed a complete schedule for biometric exit implementation.[22] In September 2008, we further reported that DHS was unlikely to meet its timeline for implementing an air exit system with biometric indicators, such as fingerprints, by July 1, 2009, because of several unresolved issues, such as opposition to the department's published plan by the airline industry.[23] In November 2009, we found that DHS had not adopted an integrated approach to scheduling, executing, and tracking the work that needed to be accomplished to deliver a comprehensive exit solution.[24] In our prior reports, we have made recommendations intended to help ensure that biometric exit was planned, designed, developed, and implemented in an effective and efficient manner. DHS generally agreed with our recommendations. DHS has implemented or taken actions to implement some of these

---

[21]8 U.S.C. § 1365b.

[22]In February 2007 and August 2007, among other things, we found that DHS had proposed spending millions of dollars on continuing operations that had known limitations and that the investments were disproportionately directed toward management-related activities. See GAO, *Homeland Security: Planned Expenditures for U.S. Visitor and Immigrant Status Program Need to Be Adequately Defined and Justified*, GAO-07-278, (Washington, D.C.: Feb. 14, 2007) and GAO-07-1065.

[23]GAO, *Visa Waiver Program: Actions Are Needed to Improve Management of the Expansion Process, and to Assess and Mitigate Program Risks*, GAO-08-967 (Washington, D.C.: Sept. 15, 2008).

[24]GAO, *Homeland Security: Key US-VISIT Components at Varying Stages of Completion, but Integrated and Reliable Schedule Needed*, GAO-10-13 (Washington, D.C.: Nov. 19, 2009).

recommendations; however, DHS has not addressed others. For example, in March 2012, DHS reported that the US-VISIT office was adopting procedures to comply with the nine scheduling practices we recommended in our November 2009 report and has conducted training on our scheduling methodology. However, DHS did not implement our February 2007 recommendations to (1) report to Congress on US-VISIT program risks associated with not fully satisfying legislative conditions, such as compliance with Office of Management and Budget capital planning and investment control guidance, and (2) limit planned expenditures for program management-related activities until such investments are economically justified and have well-defined plans.[25]

DHS Continually Reviews Records of Potential Overstays, but a Significant Number of Unmatched Arrival Records Remain

DHS Reviewed a Backlog of 1.6 Million Records of Potential Overstays in 2011

DHS reviewed a backlog of records of potential overstays that we previously identified in April 2011.[26] DHS uses ADIS to match departure records to arrival records and subsequently close records for individuals with matching arrival and departure records because either (1) the individual departed prior to the end of his or her authorized period of admission and is therefore not an overstay, or (2) the individual departed after the end of his or her authorized period of admission and is therefore an out-of-country overstay. Unmatched arrival records—those records in

---

[25]In response to our recommendation that DHS report to Congress on US-VISIT program risks, DHS did not provide us with evidence that it had reported this information to Congress. Regarding our recommendation that DHS limit planned expenditures for US-VISIT management-related activities, DHS did not complete an economic justification of its program management investments or define a detailed set of actions, milestones, and measures that would link its program management activities to program outcomes.

[26]GAO-11-411.

ADIS that do not have corresponding departure records—remain open and indicate that those individuals are potential in-country overstays.[27] In April 2011, we reported that, as of January 2011, ADIS contained a backlog of 1.6 million unmatched arrival records that DHS had not reviewed through automated or manual processes. This backlog included prior nonpriority overstay leads that had not been reviewed, nonpriority leads that continued to accrue on a daily basis, and leads generated in error as a result of CBP system changes.[28] DHS officials attributed this backlog to resource constraints and US-VISIT's focus on reviewing leads that met ICE's priorities.

In the summer of 2011, DHS completed a review of these 1.6 million records against various national security and law enforcement databases to determine if the subjects of these records had already left the United States and to help identify if the subjects posed any potential national security or public safety threats. As a result, DHS closed approximately 863,000 records for individuals who had departed, were in status, or had adjusted status, and removed them from the backlog by conducting additional automated checks. Second, DHS reviewed the remaining 757,000 records against national security and law enforcement databases to identify potential national security or public safety threats. As part of this national security and public safety review, DHS also reviewed approximately 82,000 additional records identified by CTCEU that were unresolved or had not yet undergone full review because they did not meet ICE's enforcement priorities (a total of approximately 839,000 combined records). As a result of these reviews, DHS reprioritized 1,901 of the 839,000 records because the subjects of the records could pose national security or public safety concerns and provided them to CTCEU for further review and consideration for enforcement action. Table 3 describes how CTCEU resolved these leads.

---

[27]Enforcement actions for in-country and out-of-country overstays differ in that the focus of enforcement against in-country overstays is to remove them from the country if they pose a threat, whereas enforcement against out-of-country overstays is to prevent possible readmission to the United States.

[28]ICE prioritizes potential overstay leads for possible investigation. The specific criteria ICE uses to rank the priority level of overstay leads are determined triannually based on current threat information by the Compliance Enforcement Advisory Panel, an interagency panel of intelligence experts assembled by ICE for the purpose of determining these criteria. CBP system changes had resulted in multiple arrival and departure records being inadvertently created for a single individual.

Table 3: Results of DHS's Summer 2011 Review of Nonpriority Records of Potential Overstays Identified as National Security and Public Safety Threats, as of March 2013

Outcome	Number of records (percentage of total)
Individual had departed the United States	711 records (37.4 percent)
Records forwarded to ICE's Enforcement and Removal Operations (ERO) as potential public safety threats[a]	481 records (25.3 percent)
Individual was in status (e.g., the subject filed a timely application to change his or her status or extend his or her authorized period of admission in the United States)	302 records (15.9 percent)
Individual could not be located[b]	266 records (14.0 percent)
Individual was arrested	9 records (0.5 percent)
Other[c]	132 records (6.9 percent)
Total	**1,901 records (100 percent)**

Source: ICE CTCEU.

[a]CTCEU refers information on nonpriority potential overstays to ICE's ERO, which is responsble for identifying and apprehending aliens who are subject to removal from the country, detaining these individuals when necessary, and removing aliens subject to removal from the United States. ERO personnel may encounter overstays in the course of their work but they do not directly focus on overstay enforcement.

[b]An ICE contractor's system automatically queries these records against various databases on a weekly basis for new information relating to the location of the suspected overstay. If such information is identified, CTCEU will reopen the investigation.

[c]Other includes the following outcomes: (1) ICE determined that information indicating a possble national security or public safety threat was false (73 leads, 3.8 percent); (2) the subject of the lead was in removal proceedings, previously arrested, or the subject of an investigation (43 leads, 2.3 percent); (3) the lead is open for continuous review (13 leads, 0.7 percent); and (4) the subject of the lead is the subject of an ongoing investigation at an ICE Homeland Security Investigations field office (3 leads, 0.2 percent).

According to our analysis of DHS documentation, since completing this review of the backlog of records of potential overstays in the summer of 2011, as new records have accrued, DHS has continued to review all records of potential overstays through national security and law enforcement databases to identify potential threats, regardless of whether the subjects of the records meet ICE's priorities for enforcement action. DHS also regularly rereviews these records using various national security and law enforcement databases to identify new information on individuals who were not previously identified as threats.

ICE's continual review of records of potential overstays enables it to prioritize and investigate individuals who pose a potential national security or public safety threat; however, most records of potential overstays do not result in enforcement action because they do not meet HSI's overstay enforcement priorities. CTCEU provides those records that do not meet

HSI's overstay enforcement priorities for possible investigation to ICE's ERO for review to determine if the subjects of these records could be within the scope of one of ERO's programs. For example, ERO oversees the Criminal Alien Program, which seeks to identify, arrest, and remove priority aliens who are incarcerated within federal, state, and local prisons and jails. According to ERO officials, upon receiving records from CTCEU, ERO may also determine through this program that the subject of the record has committed a crime and is incarcerated or at large. In fiscal years 2011 and 2012, the number of nonpriority records of potential overstays sent to ERO (more than 420,000) was almost three times the number of priority records that CTCEU reviewed for potential homeland security investigations (about 147,000) (see app. I for additional data on ICE's enforcement actions). According to ERO officials, ERO does not initiate investigations of records of potential overstays it receives unless there is evidence at the time ERO receives the record that the subject meets ERO's priorities.[29] ERO officials stated that few records of potential overstays have met ERO's priorities.

In April 2011, we found that ICE was assessing funding and resources needed to shift more overstay enforcement responsibilities to ERO, but ICE had not established a time frame for completing that assessment. We recommended that ICE establish a target time frame for completing the assessment and use the results to inform its decision on whether to assign ERO additional responsibility for overstay enforcement. DHS concurred with our recommendation and took action to address it. In June 2011, ICE conducted a pilot study and completed its assessment later that year in which it concluded that significant resources would be required to establish ERO teams dedicated to enforcement against overstays. As a result, ICE did not change ERO's overstay enforcement responsibilities.

---

[29]ERO prioritizes the apprehension, arrest, and removal of convicted criminals; those who pose a threat to national security; fugitives; and recent border entrants.

DHS Has More than 1 Million Unmatched Arrival Records That Do Not Meet Enforcement Priorities

Since DHS conducted its review of the previous backlog in 2011, additional unmatched arrival records have accrued, and as of June 2013, DHS has more than 1 million unmatched arrival records in ADIS (that is, arrival records for which ADIS does not have a record of departure or status change), which do not meet ICE's enforcement priorities. Some of these individuals are overstays, while others have either departed or changed immigration status without an ADIS record of their departure or status change. For example, the individual may have departed via a land port of entry without providing a record of departure or the individual may have applied for immigration benefits using a different name that does not match the ADIS arrival record. DHS conducts ongoing automated reviews of these records to rule out potential national security or public safety threats should updated information become available. In certain circumstances, such as when a record of a potential overstay meets one of ICE's enforcement priorities, DHS also manually searches additional databases to locate evidence of a departure or change of status. However, DHS's automated reviews have not produced evidence that the subjects of these 1 million unmatched arrival records meet its enforcement priorities. Thus, DHS has not manually reviewed them and does not plan to take enforcement action against these individuals. Until such evidence becomes available, DHS will continue to maintain this set of unmatched records.

In November 2012, DHS's set of unmatched arrival records not manually reviewed totaled approximately 1.2 million records, and we analyzed data on these records to assess trends by admission class (e.g., tourist or temporary agricultural worker), mode of travel (i.e., air, land, or sea), and time elapsed since the travelers were expected to leave the country.[30] Our analysis of the records by admission class shows that 44 percent of the unmatched arrival records were nonimmigrants who traveled to the United States on a tourist visa, while 43 percent were tourists admitted to the country under the Visa Waiver Program. Figure 1 presents our analysis of unmatched arrival records by admission class.

---

[30]Travelers from Canada or Mexico who present certain documents upon arrival may not be included in this data set because their arrivals may not be recorded in ADIS. For example, the arrivals of Canadian legal permanent residents who travel with a Canadian legal permanent resident card are not recorded in ADIS. Additionally, this set of unmatched arrival records does not include individuals admitted for duration of status, such as students.

Figure 1: Analysis of Unmatched Arrival Records by Admission Class, as of November 2012

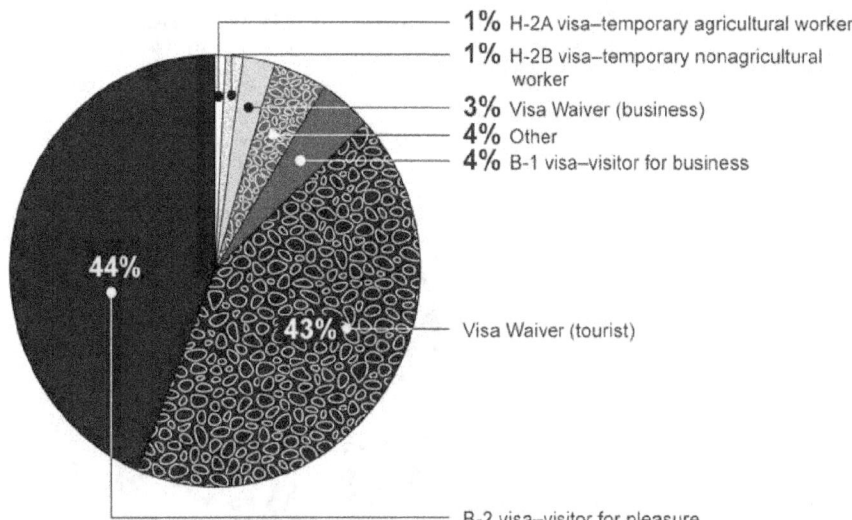

1% H-2A visa–temporary agricultural worker

1% H-2B visa–temporary nonagricultural worker

3% Visa Waiver (business)

4% Other

4% B-1 visa–visitor for business

44%

43%

Visa Waiver (tourist)

B-2 visa–visitor for pleasure

Source: GAO analysis of data from the Office of Biometric Identity Management.

Note: Other includes nonimmigrant visa categories such as temporary workers with specialty occupations and spouses and children of temporary workers. The nonimmigrant classes established by the Immigration and Nationality Act generally refer to aliens with no intention of abandoning their foreign residences, and they are each given specific designations according to regulation. The B-1 and B-2 designations refer to nonimmigrants who are visiting the United States temporarily for business or pleasure, respectively. See 8 U.S.C. § 1101(a)(15)(B). The H-2B designation refers to nonimmigrants who are coming temporarily to the United States to perform temporary, nonagricultural service or labor if unemployed persons capable of performing such service or labor cannot be found in the United States, and the H-2A designation refers to nonimmigrants who are coming temporarily to the United States to perform agricultural labor or services of a temporary or seasonal nature. See 8 U.S.C. § 1101(a)(15)(H)(ii)(a)-(b). For a listing and descriptions of all nonimmigrant classes, see 8 U.S.C. § 1101(a)(15); see also 8 C.F.R. § 214.1(a)(1)-(2) for the corresponding designations. These data do not include records of nonimmigrants who are admitted for duration of status, such as students.

With regard to mode of travel, our analysis of the 1.2 million unmatched arrival records from November 2012 indicates that most of the records were for air arrivals (64 percent), and roughly one-third were for land arrivals (32 percent). The remaining 4 percent of the records were for arrivals by sea. Figure 2 presents the results of this analysis. DHS has reported a similar distribution for modes of travel for nonimmigrants arriving in fiscal years 2010 and 2011—roughly one-third by land and two-thirds by other modes, which would include air and sea arrivals.[31]

Figure 2: Analysis of Unmatched Arrival Records by Transportation Mode, as of November 2012

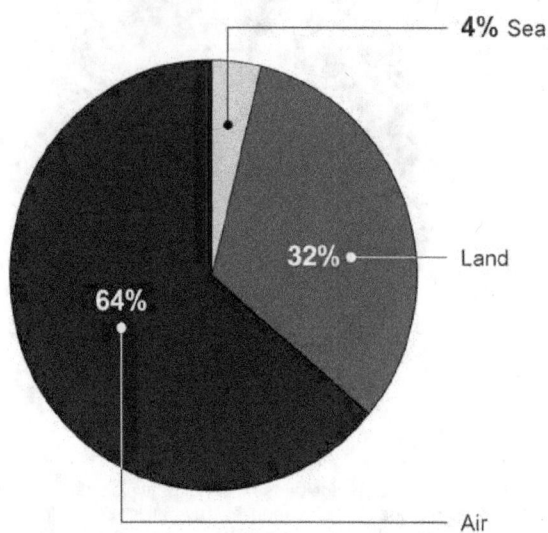

Source: GAO analysis of data from the Office of Biometric Identity Management.

We also analyzed the records to assess the amount of time that has elapsed since travelers were expected to depart the country, based on travelers' admit until date. Figure 3 presents our analysis of the amount of time elapsed, as of November 2012, since the admit until date. The average amount of time elapsed for the unmatched arrival records we analyzed was 2.7 years. Our analysis indicates that the majority of unmatched arrival records correspond to travelers who were expected to depart within the past 2 years. According to DHS officials, this may reflect that overstays are more likely to depart the United States as time

---

[31]DHS Office of Immigration Statistics, *Nonimmigrant Admissions to the United States: 2011*, (Washington, D.C.: July 2012). These data are limited to nonimmigrants for whom CBP maintains arrival/departure forms (I-94/I-94W). Mexican nationals with border crossing cards (when traveling within the border zone for a limited duration) and tourists and business travelers from Canada are generally not required to provide arrival/departure forms to CBP.

proceeds. For example, the overstays may choose to return to their countries of origin.

Figure 3: Amount of Time Elapsed since Travelers Were Expected to Depart the United States, as of November 2012, Based on Analysis of Unmatched Arrival Records

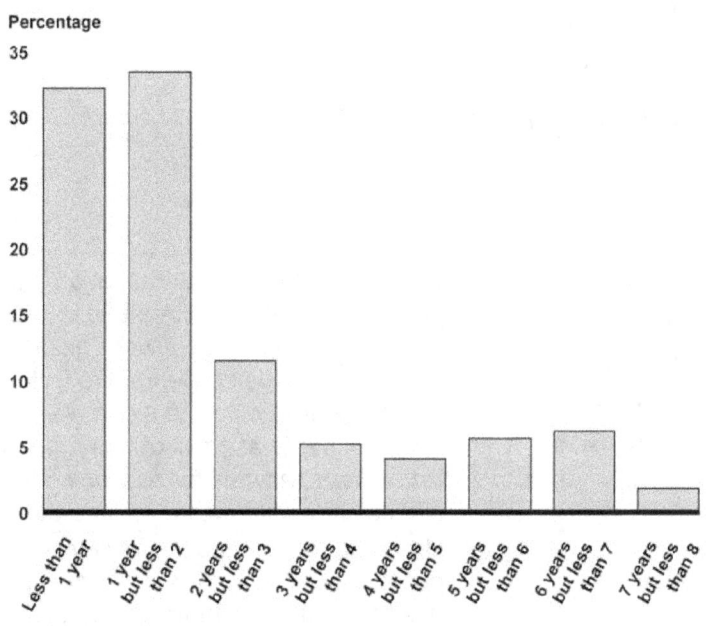

Source: GAO analysis of data from the Office of Biometric Identity Management.

GAO-13-683 Overstay Enforcement

DHS Has Actions Completed and Under Way to Improve Data to Identify Potential Overstays, but the Effect of These Improvements Is Not Yet Known

DHS Has Begun Collecting Additional Data and Improved Sharing of Data among Its Databases to Help Identify Potential Overstays

Since April 2011, DHS has taken various actions to improve its data on potential overstays. In April 2011, we found that DHS's efforts to identify and report on overstays were hindered by unreliable data, and we identified various challenges to DHS's efforts to identify potential overstays, including the incomplete collection of departure data from nonimmigrants at ports of entry, particularly land ports of entry, and the lack of mechanisms for assessing the quality of leads sent to HSI field offices for investigation.[32] Since that time, DHS has taken action to strengthen its processes for reviewing records to identify potential overstays, including (1) streamlining connections among DHS databases used to identify potential overstays and (2) collecting information from the Canadian government about those exiting the United States and entering Canada through northern land ports of entry.

First, DHS has taken steps to improve connections among its component agencies' databases used to identify potential overstays and reduce the need for manual exchanges of data. For example:

- In August 2012, DHS enhanced data sharing between ADIS and a U.S. Citizenship and Immigration Services database, the Computer-Linked Application Information Management System 3 (CLAIMS), to enable automatic transfers of immigration status or benefits information from CLAIMS to ADIS. For example, this enhancement has enabled CLAIMS to automatically provide data to ADIS when an

---

[32]GAO-11-411.

individual files a work authorization application form with U.S. Citizenship and Immigration Services, and CLAIMS also provides data to ADIS daily on whether an application is pending, approved, or denied.

- In August 2012, DHS enhanced data sharing between ADIS and IDENT. This improved connection provides additional data to ADIS to improve the matching process based on fingerprint identification. For example, when an individual provides a fingerprint as part of an application for immigration benefits from U.S. Citizenship and Immigration Services or a visa from the State Department, or when apprehended by law enforcement, IDENT now sends identity information, including a fingerprint identification number, for that individual to ADIS. This additional source of data is intended to help allow ADIS to more effectively match the individual's entry record with a change of status, thereby closing out more unmatched arrival records.

- Beginning in April 2013, ICE's Student and Exchange Visitor Information System (SEVIS) began automatically sending data to ADIS on a daily basis, allowing ADIS to review SEVIS records against departure records and determine whether student visa holders who have ended their course of study departed in accordance with the terms of their stay.[33] Prior to this date, DHS manually transferred data from SEVIS to ADIS on a weekly basis. According to DHS officials, these exchanges were unreliable because they did not consistently include all SEVIS data—particularly data on "no show" students who failed to begin their approved course of study within 30 days of being admitted into the United States.

- Also in April 2013, DHS automated the exchange of records of potential overstays between ADIS and CBP's Automated Targeting System (ATS), a CBP system used to improve the collection, use, analysis, and dissemination of information on terrorism and other violations of United States laws. This exchange is intended to allow DHS to more efficiently (1) transfer data between the systems for the purpose of identifying national security and public safety concerns, and (2) use matching algorithms in ATS that differ from those in ADIS to close additional records for individuals who departed.

---

[33]SEVIS contains biographical and other information for nonimmigrant foreign students and exchange visitors.

Second, DHS is implementing the Beyond the Border initiative to collect additional data to strengthen the identification of potential overstays. In October 2012, DHS and the Canada Border Services Agency began exchanging entry data on travelers crossing the border at selected land ports of entry. Because an entry into Canada constitutes a departure from the United States, DHS will be able to use Canadian entry data as proxies for U.S. departure records. We found in April 2011 that DHS faced challenges in its ability to identify overstays because of unreliable collection of departure data at land ports of entry.[34] The Beyond the Border Initiative would help address those challenges by providing a new source of data on travelers departing the United States at land ports on the northern border. In the pilot phase, DHS exchanged data with the Canada Border Services Agency on third-country nationals at four of the five largest ports of entry on the northern border.[35] These data covered entries from September 30, 2012, through January 15, 2013. DHS's analysis of the 413,222 records received through the pilot showed that DHS was able to match 97.4 percent of Canadian entry records to a U.S. entry record in ADIS. DHS was able to use Canadian entry records to verify the departure of approximately 11,400 subjects prior to the end of their authorized period of admission who would otherwise have been thought to be potential overstays. DHS determined that roughly 4,300 subjects with indeterminate status (meaning that DHS lacked exit records for those individuals) had left the United States after their authorized period of admission, meaning that they had overstayed while in the United States and are now considered out-of-country overstays.

DHS plans to expand this effort to collect data from additional ports of entry and to share data on additional types of travelers. Specifically, according to DHS officials, as of June 30, 2013, DHS began exchanging data for third-country nationals at all automated ports of entry along the

---

[34]GAO-11-411.

[35]These ports were Pacific Highway (Blaine, Washington), Peace Arch (Blaine, Washington), Lewiston-Queenston Bridge (Lewiston, New York), and Rainbow Bridge (Niagara Falls, New York). For the purposes of this pilot, third-country nationals are individuals who are not citizens of Canada or citizens or nationals of the United States. The pilot phase included the exchange of biographic data on permanent residents of Canada and lawful permanent residents of the United States.

northern border.[36] During this phase of the initiative, in accordance with the agreement between the United States and Canada, DHS also plans to begin using these data for operational purposes (e.g., taking enforcement action against overstays, such as working with the State Department to have their visas revoked or imposing bars on readmission to the country based on the length of time they remained in the country unlawfully).[37] After June 30, 2014, DHS plans to exchange data on all travelers, including U.S. and Canadian citizens, at all automated ports of entry along the northern border. Both DHS and Canadian officials with whom we spoke stated that the initiative is proceeding on schedule.

The Beyond the Border initiative provides DHS with additional data that should enable it to close out potential overstay leads for individuals who depart across the northern border; however, according to DHS and CBP officials, the southern land border poses unique challenges that make an approach similar to Beyond the Border difficult to implement there. Mexican entry procedures differ from those in Canada. For example, according to DHS officials, at some border crossings, Mexican officials may not collect entry data until travelers reach a station located miles past the border. Therefore, Mexican border authorities may not collect information on every traveler entering Mexico. In addition, according to DHS officials, Mexican information technology systems may be less compatible with U.S. systems than are the Canadian systems. DHS is conducting informal outreach to the Mexican government regarding the potential to share entry data in the future, but according to DHS officials, such a program would be years away.

---

[36]For the purposes of the Beyond the Border initiative, an automated port of entry refers to a port of entry on the shared Canada-U.S. land border with a primary processing capacity to capture traveler (land, ferry, and pedestrian) passage as an electronic record. This does not include large cruise vessels deemed to be sea crossings under the laws of Canada and the United States.

[37]Since these data include only individuals who have departed the United States, all of the overstays identified would be out-of-country overstays.

DHS Continues to Face Limitations in Reporting Reliable Overstay Rates and Has Not Assessed and Documented Improvements in Reliability

Since 1994, neither DHS nor its predecessor has regularly reported annual overstay rates to Congress because of concerns about the reliability of the department's overstay data. According to statute, DHS is to submit an annual report to Congress providing numerical estimates of the number of aliens from each country in each nonimmigrant classification who overstayed an authorized period of admission that expired during the fiscal year prior to the year for which the report is made.[38] Overstay rates are among the statutory criteria that determine a participant's termination from the Visa Waiver Program.[39] Therefore, we have previously concluded that reliable and valid estimates of the number of overstays are important to manage the program.[40] In April 2011, we reported that DHS officials stated that the department had not reported overstay estimates because it had not had sufficient confidence in the quality of its overstay data. DHS officials stated at the time that, as a result, the department could not reliably report overstay estimates in accordance with the statute.[41]

In February 2013, the Secretary of Homeland Security testified that DHS plans to report overstay estimates by December 2013.[42] However, as of June 2013, DHS has not made a final determination for how it plans to calculate, report, and characterize the limitations of these data. For example, according to officials from ICE and DHS's Office of Policy, the department has calculated preliminary overstay estimates for fiscal year

---

[38]8 U.S.C. § 1376(b).

[39]See 8 U.S.C. § 1187(f). A country must be terminated from the Visa Waiver Program if that country's disqualification rate for the most recent fiscal year for which data are available was more than 3.5 percent. The disqualification rate is the total for a given fiscal year of (1) those nationals of the country who were admitted as nonimmigrant visitors and violated the terms of their admission—this would include overstays—and (2) the number of foreign nationals who were denied admission upon arrival in the United States, as it compares with the total number of nationals of that country who applied for admission as nonimmigrant visitors during the same time period. According to the statute, the country must be terminated at the beginning of the second fiscal year following the fiscal year in which the determination of the disqualification rate was made.

[40]GAO, *Illegal Immigration: INS Overstay Estimation Methods Need Improvement*, GAO/PEMD-95-20 (Washington, D.C.: Sept. 26, 1995).

[41]GAO-11-411.

[42]See testimony of Janet Napolitano, Secretary, Department of Homeland Security, before the Committee on the Judiciary, United States Senate, Washington, D.C.: February 13, 2013.

2012 and the first half of fiscal year 2013 for all travelers and classes of admission at all air, land and sea ports of entry. DHS has also calculated overstay rates by country for these time periods by determining the number of overstays (in-country plus out-of-country) divided by the total number of confirmed nonimmigrants arrivals (who were expected to depart during the identified period). However, the department is still in the process of determining what methodology it will use to generate the data it plans to report by the end of the year. In addition, DHS officials stated that the department has not yet determined whether to report data from fiscal year 2012 or fiscal year 2013, and whether to report certain overstay data publicly.

Moreover, DHS continues to face challenges in ensuring the reliability of its overstay data. In September 2008, we reported on limitations in overstay data that affect the reliability of overstay rates, such as weaknesses in departure data. We recommended that the Secretary of Homeland Security explore cost-effective actions necessary to further improve, validate, and test the reliability of overstay data.[43] DHS concurred with this recommendation and has explored actions to improve overstay data, as discussed above, but has not yet validated or tested their reliability. According to DHS Office of Policy officials, the department is better positioned than in the past to describe the limitations in the overstay data. However, challenges to reporting reliable overstay estimates remain. Although DHS has improved connections among its various databases used to help identify potential overstays, these improvements do not address some of the underlying data quality and reliability issues we previously identified. For example, in April 2011, we found that DHS faced challenges in collecting accurate and complete information from nonimmigrants departing the United States through land ports of entry. The Beyond the Border initiative is intended to help address this issue by collecting proxy data on individuals exiting from the United States at northern border ports of entry; however, DHS has not yet identified mechanisms for collecting data on individuals exiting through southern border ports of entry.

Further, inaccuracies in passenger data provided by air carriers may lead to incorrect records of potential overstays if passengers' departures are not accurately recorded. For example, according to CBP officials, CBP

---

[43]GAO-08-967.

learned in early 2011 that some carriers were inadvertently transmitting passenger data without properly recording the passengers' departure after DHS noticed an increase in the number of potential overstays. According to these officials, the issue was resolved in April 2011, but because of the errors in the data, an unknown number of those passengers were incorrectly identified as potential overstays. Moreover, DHS Office of Policy and ICE officials stated that, prior to the April 2013 improvements between ADIS and SEVIS, ADIS was receiving limited information on foreign students; therefore, the overstay estimates prior to April 2013 do not fully account for the extent to which foreign students in the United States were in legal status in the country. These limitations in overstay data may affect DHS's ability to report reliable overstay estimates unless resolved. Estimates of in-country overstays are based on ADIS's identification of unmatched arrival records for individuals who were expected to depart during a given year. As discussed earlier in this report, DHS does not manually review all unmatched arrival records in ADIS because many do not meet ICE's enforcement priorities. Therefore, the reliability of data in ADIS may affect the accuracy of year-end overstay statistics.

DHS has documented the results of receiving new departure data in the pilot phase of the Beyond the Border initiative to demonstrate how DHS may be able to close out more records of potential overstays in the future. However, DHS has not assessed and documented how its changes to database connections have improved the reliability of its data for the purposes of reporting overstay rate calculations and has not analyzed the incremental improvements that database changes have made in data quality. According to DHS Office of Policy and ICE officials, DHS has not conducted such an analysis because it is difficult to pull such data from ADIS. DHS has not maintained a separate, mirrored system of ADIS and must therefore pull data directly from the live ADIS system—a resource-intensive process that can take several months. However, there may be other cost-effective ways to assess data improvements, such as conducting quantitative analyses of the number of records closed as a result of the improvements in connections among databases.

Standards for Internal Control in the Federal Government states that program managers need operational data to determine whether they are meeting their goals for accountability for effective and efficient use of resources. The standards also require that all transactions be clearly documented in a manner that is complete and accurate in order to be useful for managers and others involved in evaluating operations.[44] Additionally, GAO's methodology transfer paper on the logic of program evaluation designs, which describes key issues in evaluating federal programs, states that the basic components of an evaluation design include identifying information sources and measures, data collection methods, and an assessment of study limitations, among other things.[45] Moreover, GAO's standards for assessing computer-processed data, which can provide a framework for assessing DHS's computer-processed overstay data, states that care should be taken to ensure that collected data are sufficient and appropriate. Data may not be sufficiently reliable if (1) significant errors or incompleteness exists in some of or all the key data elements, and (2) using the data would probably lead to an incorrect or unintentional message.[46] Without an assessment and documentation of improvements in the reliability of the data used to develop overstay estimates and any remaining limitations in how the data can be used, decision makers will not have the information needed to use these data for policy-making purposes.

DHS Faces Long-standing Challenges and Uncertain Time Frames in Planning for a Biometric Exit System at Airports

DHS has not yet fulfilled the 2004 statutory requirement to implement a biometric exit capability, but has planning efforts under way to report to Congress in time for the fiscal year 2016 budget cycle on the costs and benefits of such a capability at airports and seaports. In 2004, the Intelligence Reform and Terrorism Prevention Act required DHS to develop a plan to accelerate full implementation of an automated biometric entry and exit system at air, sea, and land ports of entry. However, development and implementation of a biometric exit capability has been a long-standing challenge for DHS. With regard to an exit capability at airports, in an October 2010 memo, DHS identified three primary reasons why it has been unable to determine how and when to implement a biometric solution: (1) the methods of collecting biometric data could disrupt the flow of travelers through air terminals; (2) air carriers and airport authorities had not allowed DHS to examine mechanisms through which DHS could incorporate biometric data

---

[44]GAO/AIMD-00-21.3.1.

[45]GAO-12-208G.

[46]GAO-09-680G.

collection into passenger processing at the departure gate; and (3) challenges existed in capturing biometric data at the point of departure, including determining what personnel should be responsible for the capture of biometric information at airports. With regard to an exit capability at land ports of entry, in 2006, we reported that according to DHS officials, for various reasons, a biometric exit capability could not be implemented without incurring a major impact on land facilities.[47] As a result, as of April 2013, according to DHS officials, the department's planning efforts focus on developing a biometric exit capability for airports, with the potential for a similar solution to be implemented at seaports, and DHS's planning documents, as of June 2013, do not address plans for a biometric exit capability at land ports of entry.

According to DHS officials, the challenges DHS identified in October 2010 continue to affect the department's ability to implement a biometric air exit system. For example, in 2009, DHS conducted pilot programs for biometric air exit capabilities in airport scenarios.[48] In August 2010, we found that there were limitations with the pilot programs—for example, the pilot programs did not operationally test about 30 percent of the air exit requirements identified in the evaluation plan for the pilot programs—that hindered DHS's ability to inform decision making for a long-term air exit solution and pointed to the need for additional sources of information on air exit's operational impacts.[49] According to DHS officials, the

---

[47]GAO, *Border Security: US-VISIT Program Faces, Strategic, Operational, and Technological Challenges at Land Ports of Entry*, GAO-07-248 (Washington, D.C.: Dec. 6, 2006).

[48]In April 2008, DHS announced its intention to implement biometric exit verification at air and sea ports of entry in a Notice of Proposed Rule Making (73 Fed. Reg. 22065 (Apr. 24, 2008)). Under this notice, commercial air and sea carriers would be respons ble for developing and deploying the capability to collect the biometrics from departing travelers and transmit them to DHS. Subsequent to the rule making notice, on September 30, 2008, the Consolidated Security, Disaster Assistance, and Continuing Appropriations Act, 2009, was enacted, which directed DHS to test two scenarios for an air exit solution. (Pub. L. No. 110-329, 122 Stat. 3574, 3668-70 (2008).) The act prohibited DHS from obligating any US-VISIT funds provided in the act for the implementation of an air exit solution until the department provided a report to the Senate and House Committees on Appropriations on pilot tests for the solution that addressed two scenarios: CBP collects biometric exit data at airport departure gates; and airlines collect and transmit such data. DHS submitted its Air Exit Pilots Evaluation Report to the House and Senate Appropriations Subcommittees on Homeland Security in October 2009.

[49]GAO, *Homeland Security: US-VISIT Pilot Evaluations Offer Limited Understanding of Air Exit Options*, GAO-10-860 (Washington, D.C.: Aug. 10, 2010).

department's approach to planning for biometric air exit since that time has been partly in response to our recommendation that DHS identify additional sources for the operational impacts of air exit not addressed in the pilot programs' evaluation and to incorporate these sources into its air exit decision making and planning. Figure 4 depicts a timeline of DHS's efforts to develop a biometric exit capability and key findings from our prior reports.

Interactive graphic **Figure 4: Timeline of Events Related to Biometric Entry and Exit System**

Move mouse over the blue shaded text boxes to get more information on GAO's findings and recommendation, click on text box to open the referenced GAO report. For an accessible and printable version of this graphic please see appendix II.

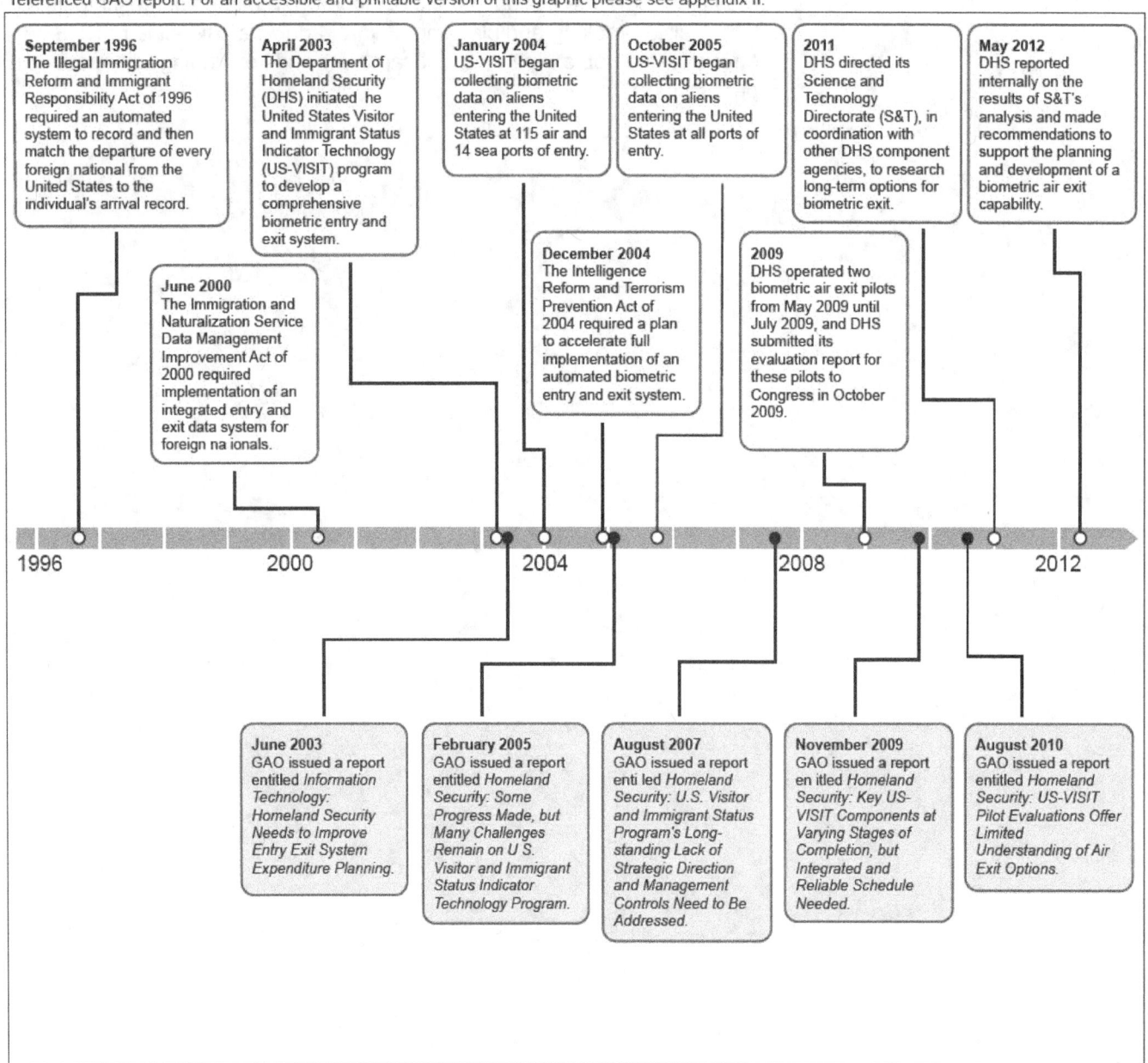

September 1996
The Illegal Immigration Reform and Immigrant Responsibility Act of 1996 required an automated system to record and then match the departure of every foreign national from the United States to the individual's arrival record.

April 2003
The Department of Homeland Security (DHS) initiated he United States Visitor and Immigrant Status Indicator Technology (US-VISIT) program to develop a comprehensive biometric entry and exit system.

January 2004
US-VISIT began collecting biometric data on aliens entering the United States at 115 air and 14 sea ports of entry.

October 2005
US-VISIT began collecting biometric data on aliens entering the United States at all ports of entry.

2011
DHS directed its Science and Technology Directorate (S&T), in coordination with other DHS component agencies, to research long-term options for biometric exit.

May 2012
DHS reported internally on the results of S&T's analysis and made recommendations to support the planning and development of a biometric air exit capability.

June 2000
The Immigration and Naturalization Service Data Management Improvement Act of 2000 required implementation of an integrated entry and exit data system for foreign na ionals.

December 2004
The Intelligence Reform and Terrorism Prevention Act of 2004 required a plan to accelerate full implementation of an automated biometric entry and exit system.

2009
DHS operated two biometric air exit pilots from May 2009 until July 2009, and DHS submitted its evaluation report for these pilots to Congress in October 2009.

1996   2000   2004   2008   2012

June 2003
GAO issued a report entitled *Information Technology: Homeland Security Needs to Improve Entry Exit System Expenditure Planning.*

February 2005
GAO issued a report entitled *Homeland Security: Some Progress Made, but Many Challenges Remain on U S. Visitor and Immigrant Status Indicator Technology Program.*

August 2007
GAO issued a report enti led *Homeland Security: U.S. Visitor and Immigrant Status Program's Long-standing Lack of Strategic Direction and Management Controls Need to Be Addressed.*

November 2009
GAO issued a report en itled *Homeland Security: Key US-VISIT Components at Varying Stages of Completion, but Integrated and Reliable Schedule Needed.*

August 2010
GAO issued a report entitled *Homeland Security: US-VISIT Pilot Evaluations Offer Limited Understanding of Air Exit Options.*

Source: GAO.

In 2011, DHS directed S&T, in coordination with other DHS component agencies, to research long-term options for biometric air exit.[50] In May 2012, DHS reported internally on the results of S&T's analysis of previous air exit pilot programs and assessment of available technologies, and the report made recommendations to support the planning and development of a biometric air exit capability.[51] In that report, DHS concluded that the building blocks to implement an effective biometric air exit system were available. In addition, DHS's report stated that new traveler facilitation tools and technologies—for example, online check-in, self-service, and paperless technology—could support more cost-effective ways to screen travelers, and that these improvements should be leveraged when developing plans for biometric air exit. However, DHS officials stated that there may be challenges to leveraging new technologies to the extent that U.S. airports and airlines rely on older, proprietary systems that may be difficult to update to incorporate new technologies. Furthermore, DHS reported in May 2012 that significant questions remained regarding (1) the effectiveness of current biographic air exit processes and the error rates in collecting or matching data, (2) methods of cost-effectively integrating biometrics into the air departure processes (e.g., collecting biometric scans as passengers enter the jetway to board a plane), (3) the additional value biometric air exit would provide compared with the current biographic air exit process, and (4) the overall value and cost of a biometric air exit capability. The report included nine recommendations to help inform DHS's planning for biometric air exit, such as directing DHS to develop explicit goals and objectives for biometric air exit and an evaluation framework that would, among other things, assess the value of

---

[50]In our previous reviews of DHS's efforts to pursue biometric exit capabilities, DHS's plans have approached development of a biometric exit system through a phased approach that involved conducting pilots to inform eventual planning for long-term solutions. Different pilots were created to inform solutions at air/seaports and land ports. See GAO-10-13. As of April 2013, the department's planning efforts are focused on developing a biometric exit system for airports, with the potential for a similar solution to be rolled out at seaports, according to DHS officials.

[51]DHS, *DHS Biometric Air Exit: Analysis, Recommendations and Next Steps*, (Washington, D.C.: May 2012).

collecting biometric data in addition to biographic data and determine whether biometric air exit is economically justified.[52]

DHS reported in May 2012 that it planned to take steps to address these recommendations by May 2014; however, according to DHS Office of Policy and S&T officials, the department does not expect to fully address these recommendations by then. In particular, DHS officials stated that it has been difficult coordinating with airlines and airports, which have expressed reluctance about biometric air exit because of concerns over its effect on operations and potential costs. To address these concerns, DHS is conducting outreach and soliciting information from airlines and airports regarding their operations. In addition, DHS officials stated that the department's efforts to date have been hindered by insufficient funding. However, in fiscal year 2012, DHS requested that Congress release funds allocated to the biometric exit program and funds being withheld pending the full implementation of a biometric exit system so that these funds could be applied to DHS's efforts to enhance the biographic exit system. In its fiscal year 2014 budget request for S&T, DHS requested funding for a joint S&T-CBP Air Entry/Exit Re-Engineering Apex project. Apex projects are crosscutting, multidisciplinary efforts requested by DHS components that are high-priority projects intended to solve problems of strategic operational importance. According to DHS's fiscal year 2014 budget justification, the Air Entry/Exit Re-Engineering Apex project will develop tools to model and simulate air entry and exit operational processes. Using these tools, DHS intends to develop, test, pilot, and evaluate candidate solutions. As of April 2013, DHS Policy and S&T officials stated that they expect to finalize goals and objectives for a biometric air exit system in the near future and are making plans for future scenario-based testing.

---

[52]The report recommended that DHS take the following actions: (1) develop explicit goals and objectives for biometric air exit, (2) leverage improvements in passenger facilitation and biometric technology to support a concept of operations, (3) use developmental scenario testing instead of pilot programs to validate a concept of operations, (4) establish collaborative relationships with airports and airlines, (5) use operational tests to validate performance and cost estimates, (6) develop an evaluation framework for biometric air exit, (7) employ a holistic approach to assess the costs and benefits of comprehensive biometric entry and exit processes, (8) determine whether biometric air exit is economically justified, and (9) incrementally deploy biometric air exit to airports where it is cost-effective to do so.

Although DHS's May 2012 report stated that DHS would take steps to address the report's recommendations by May 2014, DHS officials told us that the department's current goal is to develop information about options for biometric air exit and to report to Congress in time for the fiscal year 2016 budget cycle regarding (1) the additional benefits that a biometric air exit system provides beyond an enhanced biographic exit system and (2) costs associated with biometric air exit. However, DHS has not yet developed an evaluation framework, as recommended in its May 2012 report, to determine how the department will evaluate the benefits and costs of a biometric air exit system and compare it with a biographic exit system. According to DHS officials, the department needs to finalize goals and objectives for biometric air exit before it can develop such a framework, and in April 2013 these officials told us that the department plans to finalize these elements in the near future. However, DHS does not have time frames for when it will subsequently be able to develop and implement an evaluation framework to support the assessment it plans to provide to Congress.

According to *A Guide to the Project Management Body of Knowledge*, which provides standards for project managers, specific goals and objectives should be conceptualized, defined, and documented in the planning process, along with the appropriate steps, time frames, and milestones needed to achieve those results.[53] In fall 2012, DHS developed a high-level plan for its biometric air exit efforts, which it updated in May 2013, but this plan does not clearly identify the tasks needed to develop and implement an evaluation framework. For example, the plan does not include a step for developing the methodology for comparing the costs and benefits of biometric data against those for collecting biographic data, as recommended in DHS's May 2012 report. Furthermore, the time frames in this plan are not accurate as of June 2013 because DHS is behind schedule on some of the tasks and has not updated the time frames in the plan accordingly. For example, DHS had planned to begin scenario-based testing for biometric air exit options in August 2013; however, according to DHS officials, the department now plans to begin such testing in early 2014. A senior official from DHS's

---

[53]Project Management Institute, *A Guide to the Project Management Body of Knowledge (PMBOK® Guide), Fifth Edition,* (Newton Square, PA: 2013). We have used *A Guide to the Project Management Body of Knowledge* to provide criteria in previous reports, including GAO, *Nonproliferation and Disarmament Fund: State Should Better Assure the Effective Use of Program Authorities,* GAO-13-83 (Washington, D.C.: Nov. 30, 2012).

Office of Policy told us that DHS has not kept the plan up to date because of the transition of responsibilities within DHS; specifically, in March 2013, pursuant to the explanatory statement for DHS's 2013 appropriation, DHS established an office within CBP that is responsible for coordinating DHS's entry and exit policies and operations.[54] This transition was in process as of June 2013, and CBP plans to establish an integrated project team in July 2013 that will be responsible for more detailed planning for the department's biometric air exit efforts. Without robust planning that includes up-to-date time frames and milestones to develop and implement an evaluation framework for its assessment of biometric air exit benefits and costs, DHS does not have reasonable assurance that it will be able to provide this assessment to Congress as planned for the fiscal year 2016 budget cycle.

DHS Policy and S&T officials agreed that setting time frames and milestones is important to ensure timely development and implementation of the evaluation framework in accordance with DHS's May 2012 recommendations. According to DHS officials, implementation of a biometric air exit system will depend on the results of discussions between the department and Congress after the department provides this assessment of options for biometric air exit. Any delays in providing the assessment to Congress could further affect implementation of a biometric air exit system, and without reasonable assurance when DHS will be able to provide this assessment to Congress, it remains unclear when DHS will make progress toward addressing the statutory requirements for a biometric exit system.

Conclusions

Addressing the large number of foreign visitors who have entered the United States legally but then overstayed has been a long-standing challenge. Given the government's finite resources for addressing overstays, and competing priorities, reliable data and analysis are of particular importance to both DHS and Congress. Without clear assessment and reporting of the extent to which the reliability of the data used to develop overstay estimates has improved and any remaining limitations in how the data can be used, decision makers may not have complete information needed to use these data for policy-making

---

[54]See Explanatory Statement, Consolidated and Further Continuing Appropriations Act, 2013, 159 Cong. Rec. S1287, S1550 (daily ed. Mar. 11, 2013).

purposes. Furthermore, DHS has faced long-standing challenges in making progress toward meeting the statutory requirement for biometric exit capabilities since 2004. DHS plans to provide Congress with an assessment of the benefits and costs of various options for pursuing a biometric exit system at airports, but without robust planning that includes time frames and milestones to develop and implement an evaluation framework for this assessment, DHS lacks reasonable assurance that it will be able to provide this assessment to Congress for the fiscal year 2016 budget cycle as planned. Furthermore, any delays in providing this information to Congress could further affect possible implementation of a biometric exit system to address statutory requirements.

Recommendations for Executive Action

To help improve confidence in the quality of overstay data that DHS plans to report in December 2013 in accordance with statutory reporting requirements, we recommend that the Secretary of Homeland Security direct relevant DHS components to assess and document the extent to which the reliability of the data used to develop any overstay estimates has improved and any remaining limitations in how the data can be used.

To provide reasonable assurance of when DHS will be able provide an assessment of the benefits and costs of biometric air exit options to Congress, we recommend that the Secretary of Homeland Security establish time frames and milestones for developing and implementing an evaluation framework to be used in conducting the department's assessment of biometric air exit options.

Agency Comments and Our Evaluation

We provided a draft of this report to DHS and the Department of State for their review and comment. DHS provided written comments, which are summarized below and reproduced in full in appendix III. DHS concurred with our two recommendations and described actions under way or planned to address them. Regarding our first recommendation, that DHS assess and document the extent to which the reliability of the data used to develop any overstay estimates has improved and any remaining limitations in how the data can be used, DHS indicated that it is establishing a working group that will include representation from DHS component agencies with responsibility for collecting, recording, and analyzing entry and exit data and that this working group will be functional by January 31, 2014. According to DHS, the component agencies that oversee information systems used to identify overstays will be responsible for the data captured in their respective systems, and the working group will be responsible for aggregating information across components regarding the validity of the data and defining any limitations to the use of the data. DHS estimated that completion of an initial evaluation of the data would occur by July 31, 2014. To fully address our recommendation, DHS should assess the reliability of, and document any remaining limitations in, any overstay data that the department may report. Regarding our second recommendation, that DHS establish time frames and milestones for developing and implementing an evaluation framework to be used in conducting the department's assessment of biometric air exit options, DHS indicated that CBP and S&T will finalize the goals and objectives for biometric air exit by January 31, 2014, and that these goals and objectives will be used in the development of an evaluation framework that DHS expects to have completed by June 30, 2014. These actions, when fully implemented, should help address the intent of our recommendations. DHS also provided technical comments, which we incorporated as appropriate.

The Department of State did not have formal comments on our draft report, but provided technical comments, which we incorporated as appropriate.

We are sending copies of this report to the Secretary of Homeland Security, the Secretary of State, appropriate congressional committees, and other interested parties. In addition, the report is available at no charge on the GAO website at http://www.gao.gov.

If you or your staff have questions on matters discussed in this report, please contact me at (202) 512-8777 or gamblerr@gao.gov. Contact points for our Offices of Congressional Relations and Public Affairs may be found on the last page of this report. GAO staff that made major contributions to this report are listed in appendix IV.

Rebecca Gambler
Director
Homeland Security and Justice

Appendix I: U.S. Immigration and Customs Enforcement's Overstay Enforcement Actions

In April 2011, we reported that U.S. Immigration and Customs Enforcement (ICE), a component within the Department of Homeland Security (DHS), takes actions to address a small portion of the estimated overstay population because of, among other things, competing priorities. In particular, ICE's Counterterrorism and Criminal Exploitation Unit (CTCEU), within the Homeland Security Investigations (HSI) directorate, prioritizes in-country overstay leads based on various factors that consider the potential risks overstays may pose to national security and public safety, and HSI field offices investigate those leads that CTCEU identifies as priorities.

As it reviews leads for potential overstays, CTCEU closes records for nonimmigrants that have either left the country or changed their status, identifies nonpriority records for processing by ICE Enforcement and Removal Operations, and sends records that do not have a viable address to contractors to continually monitor for new address information. CTCEU assigns valid, high-priority overstay leads to HSI field office agents within their respective geographical areas of responsibility for mandatory investigation. From fiscal years 2004 through 2012, CTCEU processed over 2.2 million records of potential overstays and sent about 44,500 leads to HSI field offices for investigation. Table 4 provides information related to the records of potential overstays that CTCEU has processed from fiscal years 2004 through 2012 (our April 2011 report included the data from fiscal years 2004 through 2010). Out of the approximately 44,500 leads sent to HSI field offices over this period of time, approximately 9,000 (about 20 percent) resulted in arrests.

Table 4: U.S. Immigration and Customs Enforcement Counterterrorism and Criminal Exploitation Unit (CTCEU) Processing of Records of Potential In-Country Overstays from Fiscal Years 2004 to 2012 (Rounded to the Nearest Hundred)

Status of leads	2004	2005	2006	2007	2008	2009	2010	2011	2012	Total
Records imported	261,600	198,600	168,500	197,300	155,600	198,300	193,300	390,200	497,500	2,260,900
Closed records	239,500	180,900	148,200	166,400	104,600	101,100	103,900	169,000	233,400	1,447,000
Nonpriority records of potential overstays sent to Enforcement and Removal Operations	13,900	13,000	15,800	25,100	46,000	85,600	79,700	199,200	221,900	700, 200
Viable leads assigned to Homeland Security Investigations field offices for investigation	7,600	4,600	4,300	5,700	5,000	6,100	5,400	3,000	2,800	44,500
Nonviable leads sent to contractor for continual monitoring	700	300	300	200	100	6,000	4,900	3,000	4,400	19,900

Source: CTCEU LeadTrac data on overstay leads.

In April 2011, we reported that overstay investigations that do not lead to an arrest result in one of three outcomes: (1) evidence is uncovered indicating that the suspected overstay departed the United States, (2) evidence is uncovered indicating that the subject of the investigation is in-status (e.g., the subject filed a timely application with DHS's U.S. Citizenship and Immigration Services to change his or her status or extend his or her authorized period of admission in the United States), or (3) investigators exhaust all investigative leads and cannot locate the suspected overstay. If the evidence of departure shows that the individual departed after his or her authorized admit until date (i.e., the individual is an out-of-country overstay), the individual could be subject to administrative enforcement actions including restrictions on readmission to the United States. Figure 5 shows the outcomes of CTCEU investigations from fiscal years 2004 through 2012 that did not result in arrest (our April 2011 report included the data from fiscal years 2004 through 2010).

Figure 5: Outcomes of U.S. Immigration and Customs Enforcement
Counterterrorism and Criminal Exploitation Unit (CTCEU) Overstay Investigations
Not Resulting in Arrest, Fiscal Years 2004-2012

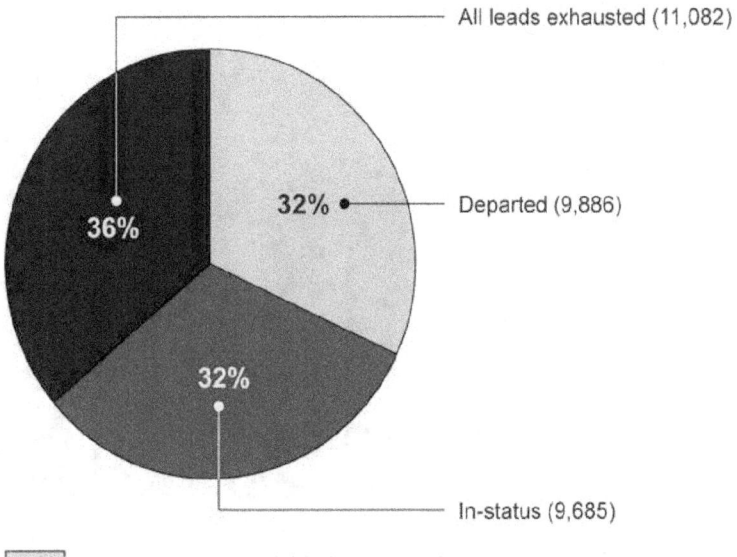

All leads exhausted (11,082)

Departed (9,886)

In-status (9,685)

36%

32%

32%

Departed, individual has departed the United States

In status, individual filed a timely application to adjust his or her authorized admission into the United States

All leads exhausted, despite taking investigative steps, agents cannot locate individual

Source: GAO analysis of CTCEU data.

Note: Data presented in this table include outcomes of CTCEU investigations of suspected visa overstays, Visa Waiver Program overstays, National Security Entry-Exit Registration System overstays, and out-of-status students. The National Security Entry-Exit Registration System was a program that required certain visitors or nonimmigrants to register with DHS for national security reasons. DHS ended this program on April 27, 2011.

As we reported in April 2011, ICE has reported allocating a small percentage of its resources in terms of investigative work hours to overstay investigations. For this report, we found that, from fiscal years 2005 through 2012, ICE reported devoting from 1.8 to 3.4 percent of its total HSI field office investigative hours to CTCEU overstay investigations, as shown in figure 6 (our April 2011 report included the data from fiscal years 2006 through 2010).

Figure 6: U.S. Immigration and Customs Enforcement (ICE) Reported Percentage of Homeland Security Investigations Field Office Investigative Hours Dedicated to Overstay Investigations, Fiscal Years 2005-2012

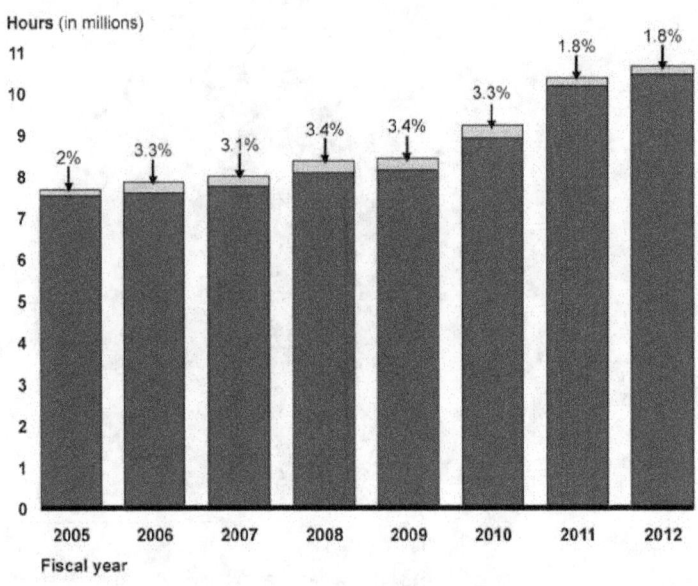

Hours (in millions)

| Field office investigative hours dedicated to overstay cases |
| Field office investigative hours dedicated to other categories of investigations |

Source: GAO analysis of ICE data.

Note: Data in this figure do not account for all categories of investigations that may result in enforcement actions against overstays. For example, these data do not include document or benefit fraud investigations, which include school fraud investigations that may identify out-of-status students.

Appendix II: Timeline of Events Related to Biometric Entry and Exit System

Table 5 lists events in DHS's efforts to develop a biometric exit capability and key findings from our prior reports (see interactive fig. 4) and includes the figure's rollover information.

Table 5: Timeline of Events Related to Biometric Entry and Exit System

Date	Event
September 1996	The Illegal Immigration Reform and Immigrant Responsibility Act of 1996 required an automated system to record and then match the departure of every foreign national from the United States to the individual's arrival record.
June 2000	The Immigration and Naturalization Service Data Management Improvement Act of 2000 required implementation of an integrated entry and exit data system for foreign nationals.
April 2003	The Department of Homeland Security (DHS) initiated the United States Visitor and Immigrant Status Indicator Technology (US-VISIT) program to develop a comprehensive biometric entry and exit system.
June 2003	GAO issued a report entitled *Information Technology: Homeland Security Needs to Improve Entry Exit System Expenditure Planning.*
	GAO findings
	GAO reported that DHS's initial plan for an entry-exit system did not provide sufficient information about specific system capabilities, benefits, and costs.
	Recommendation
	GAO recommended that the Secretary of Homeland Security ensure that future expenditure plans fully disclose what entry-exit system capabilities and benefits are to be delivered, by when, and at what cost, and how the department intends to manage the acquisition to provide reasonable assurance that these system capability, benefit, schedule, and cost commitments will be met.
	Status
	Closed–implemented
	The fiscal year 2007 expenditure plan disclosed planned system capabilities, expected benefits, and estimated schedules and costs. More specifically, the expenditure plan identified capabilities for various US-VISIT projects, such as the capability to receive and store 10-print finger scans captured by U.S. consulates. Additionally, the expenditure plan identified benefits, such as reduced information gaps and enhanced immigration and border enforcement. Furthermore, the expenditure plan provided time frames, such as the deployment of the 10-print pilot to 10 air locations in late 2007. Moreover, the expenditure plan provided meaningful cost information for some of its projects.
	GAO citation
	GAO, *Information Technology: Homeland Security Needs to Improve Entry Exit System Expenditure Planning,* GAO-03-563 (Washington, D.C.: June 9, 2003).
January 2004	US-VISIT began collecting biometric data on aliens entering the United States at 115 air and 14 sea ports of entry.
December 2004	The Intelligence Reform and Terrorism Prevention Act of 2004 required a plan to accelerate full implementation of an automated biometric entry and exit system.

Date	Event
February 2005	GAO issued a report entitled *Homeland Security: Some Progress Made, but Many Challenges Remain on U.S. Visitor and Immigrant Status Indicator Technology Program.*
	GAO findings
	GAO reported that changing facts and circumstances introduced additional risk to US-VISIT's delivery of promised capabilities and benefits on time and within budget.
	Recommendation
	GAO recommended that the Secretary of Homeland Security direct the Under Secretary for Border and Transportation Security to ensure that the US-VISIT program director reassesses plans for deploying an exit capability to ensure that the scope of the exit pilot program provides for adequate evaluation of alternative solutions and better ensures that the exit solution selected is in the best interest of the program.
	Status
	Closed–implemented
	The fiscal year 2008 expenditure plan stated that DHS reassessed its exit plans, described a new strategy for deploying biometric exit capabilities at air and sea ports of entry, and noted the absence of near-term biometric options for land ports of entry. DHS also shut down the exit pilots (and demonstration projects) that this recommendation was intended to address.
	GAO citation
	GAO, *Homeland Security: Some Progress Made, but Many Challenges Remain on U.S. Visitor and Immigrant Status Indicator Technology Program*, GAO-05-202 (Washington, D.C.: Feb. 23, 2005).
October 2005	US-VISIT began collecting biometric data on aliens entering the United States at all ports of entry.
August 2007	GAO issued a report entitled *Homeland Security: U.S. Visitor and Immigrant Status Program's Long-standing Lack of Strategic Direction and Management Controls Need to Be Addressed.*
	GAO findings
	GAO reported that DHS continued to propose spending tens of millions of dollars on US-VISIT exit projects that were not well defined, planned, or justified on the basis of costs, benefits, and risks.
	Recommendation
	In this report, GAO reiterated prior recommendations regarding the US-VISIT program and further recommended that the Secretary of Homeland Security report to the department's authorization and appropriations committees on its reasons for not fully addressing its expenditure plan legislative conditions and our prior recommendations.
	Status
	Closed–not implemented
	US-VISIT program officials told GAO that they had periodically briefed their authorization and appropriation committees on program-related issues, including reasons for not having fully satisfied all expenditure plan legislative conditions and GAO's prior recommendations. However, documentation of these congressional briefings provided by US-VISIT does not indicate that the program's reasons for not fully addressing expenditure plan legislative conditions or our open recommendations were discussed. As of August 2011, DHS officials had yet to provide evidence of discussions with the congressional committees regarding the topics of this recommendation, and GAO closed the recommendation as not implemented.
	GAO citation
	GAO, *Homeland Security: U.S. Visitor and Immigrant Status Program's Long-standing Lack of Strategic Direction and Management Controls Need to be Addressed,* GAO-07-1065 (Washington, D.C.: Aug. 31, 2007).
2009	DHS operated two biometric air exit pilots from May 2009 until July 2009, and DHS submitted its evaluation report for these pilots to Congress in October 2009.

Date	Event
November 2009	GAO issued a report entitled *Homeland Security: Key US-VISIT Components at Varying Stages of Completion, but Integrated and Reliable Schedule Needed.*

GAO findings

GAO reported that the US-VISIT program office had not adopted an integrated approach to scheduling, executing, and tracking work toward a comprehensive exit solution.

Recommendation

GAO recommended that the US-VISIT program director develop and maintain an integrated master schedule for the exit system project in accordance with nine scheduling practices discussed in the report.

Status

Open

In March 2012, DHS reported that the US-VISIT office was adopting procedures to comply with the nine scheduling practices GAO recommended and has conducted training on our scheduling methodology.

GAO citation

GAO, *Homeland Security: Key US-VISIT Components at Varying Stages of Completion, but Integrated and Reliable Schedule Needed,* GAO-10-13 (Washington, D.C.: Nov. 19, 2009). |
| August 2010 | GAO issued a report entitled *Homeland Security: US-VISIT Pilot Evaluations Offer Limited Understanding of Air Exit Options.*

GAO findings

GAO reported that DHS would need to leverage other sources of information to develop a biometric air exit solution given limitations in DHS's biometric air exit pilot programs.

Recommendation

GAO recommend that the US-VISIT program director identify additional sources for the operational impacts of air exit not addressed in the pilots' evaluation and to incorporate these sources into its air exit decision making and planning.

Status

Open

In May 2012, DHS reported internally on the results of the DHS Science and Technology Directorate's (S&T) analysis of previous US-VISIT air exit pilot programs and assessment of available biometric technologies. The report also discussed DHS's plans to take steps that have the potential to result in additional information sources to assess the operational impacts of a biometric air exit capability. However, the report also cited significant remaining questions, such as those regarding the comparative value of adding a biometric capability to the existing air exit process and the overall value and cost of a biometric air exit capability. As of April 2013, officials from DHS's Office of Policy and S&T stated that they are making plans for future scenario-based testing and are conducting outreach and soliciting information from airlines and airports regarding their operations.

GAO citation

GAO, *Homeland Security: US-VISIT Pilot Evaluations Offer Limited Understanding of Air Exit Options,* GAO-10-860 (Washington, D.C.: Aug. 10, 2010). |
| 2011 | DHS directed S&T, in coordination with other DHS component agencies, to research long-term options for biometric exit. |
| May 2012 | DHS reported internally on the results of S&T's analysis and made recommendations to support the planning and development of a biometric air exit capability. |

Source: GAO.

Appendix III: Comments from the Department of Homeland Security

U.S. Department of Homeland Security
Washington, DC 20528

Homeland Security

July 18, 2013

Rebecca Gambler
Director, Homeland Security and Justice Issues
U.S. Government Accountability Office
441 G Street, NW
Washington, DC 20548

Re: Draft Report GAO-13-683, "OVERSTAY ENFORCEMENT: Additional Actions
       Needed to Assess DHS's Data and Improve Planning for a Biometric Air Exit Program"

Dear Ms. Gambler:

Thank you for the opportunity to review and comment on this draft report. The U.S. Department of Homeland Security (DHS) appreciates the U.S. Government Accountability Office's (GAO's) work in planning and conducting its review and issuing this report.

DHS is pleased to note GAO's positive recognition of the Department's efforts to reduce a backlog of previously identified potential overstay records related to foreign visitors who have entered the United States legally but then overstayed their authorized period of admission. DHS also appreciates GAO's acknowledgement of actions already completed or underway to improve data on potential overstays. DHS remains committed to strengthening and building upon existing capabilities to better identify and report on potential overstays.

The draft report contained two recommendations, with which the Department concurs. Specifically, GAO recommended that the Secretary of Homeland Security:

Recommendation 1: To help improve confidence in the quality of overstay data that DHS plans to report in December 2013 in accordance with statutory reporting requirements, direct relevant DHS components to assess and document the extent to which the reliability of the data used to develop any overstay estimates has improved and any remaining limitations in how the data can be used.

Response: Concur. In order to meet its legislative mandate and improve overstay enforcement; DHS will create a new working group to reassess its requirements, capabilities, and risks. Given the reassignment of United States Visitor and Immigrant Status Indicator Technology (US-VISIT) responsibilities to multiple Components and the ongoing evaluation of new technologies for biometric measurement of exits, the assessment of the reliability of potential overstay data has become more complex.

As the lead agency for overstay enforcement, U.S. Immigration and Customs Enforcement's (ICE's) National Security Investigations Division will chair the working group and be responsible for aggregating the requirements needed to provide assurance that DHS has a reasonable capability to identify potential visa overstays.

Other members of the group will include those Components responsible for collecting, recording, and analyzing entry and exit data. Each Component will assess its capabilities against identified requirements and provide a risk analysis for any gaps in coverage. For those members of the working group that own an information system used to identify visa overstays, that Component will be responsible for documenting their processes, justifying resources required to generate potential overstay data, information assurance, architecture, engineering, operations, and system development.

The working group will be charged with aggregating the risk to the validity of the data, monitoring the effectiveness of the system, identifying evolving needs, and defining any limits to the use of the data. Estimated Completion Dates (ECDs): Working group fully functional by January 31, 2014; Completion of initial evaluation of data by July 31, 2014.

Recommendation 2: Establish time frames and milestones for developing and implementing an evaluation framework to be used in conducting the Department's assessment of biometric air exit options.

Response: Concur. U.S. Customs and Border Protection's (CBP's) Office of Field Operations (OFO) and the Department's Science and Technology Directorate will finalize the goals and objectives for biometric exit by January 31, 2014, which will establish the Biometric Air Exit Evaluation Framework and implementation plan. Using the biometric air exit goals and objectives, CBP OFO will establish the current performance of exit processes and categorize performance parameters that will be used to monitor improvements introduced by a biometric exit solution. The Evaluation Framework will employ a rigorous methodology to include process, outcome, and cost components. ECD: June 30, 2014.

Again, thank you for the opportunity to review and provide comments on this draft report. Technical comments were previously provided under separate cover. Please feel free to contact me if you have any questions. We look forward to working with you in the future.

Sincerely,

Jim H. Crumpacker
Director
Departmental GAO-OIG Liaison Office

2

Appendix IV: GAO Contact and Staff Acknowledgments

GAO Contact	Rebecca Gambler, (202) 512-8777 or gamblerr@gao.gov.
Staff Acknowledgments	In addition to the contact named above, Kathryn Bernet (Assistant Director), Susan Baker, Frances A. Cook, Alana Finley, Eric Hauswirth, Richard Hung, Lara Miklozek, Amanda Miller, Anthony Moran, Karl Seifert, and Ashley D. Vaughan made significant contributions to this report.